GOOD LOO HUNTING

LUKE BARCLAY

2 4 6 8 10 9 7 5 3 1

Published in 2010 by Virgin Books, an imprint of Ebury Publishing
A Random House Group Company

Copyright © Luke Barclay 2010

Design by Toby Clarke

Luke Barclay has asserted his right under the Copyright, Designs
and Patents Act 1988 to be identified as the author of this work

The Random House Group Limited Reg. No. 954009

Addresses for companies within the Random House Group can be found at
www.randomhouse.co.uk

A CIP catalogue record for this book is available from the British Library

The Random House Group Limited supports The Forest Stewardship Council (FSC), the
leading international forest certification organisation. All our titles that are printed on
Greenpeace-approved FSC-certified paper carry the FSC logo. Our paper procurement
policy can be found at www.rbooks.co.uk/environment

Printed in China by C&C Offset Printing Co. Ltd

ISBN 9780753522509

To buy books by your favourite authors and register for offers visit **www.rbooks.co.uk**

For Alice, Anna, Sam and Gabbi

Contents

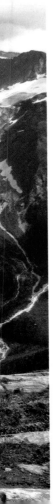

Introduction

I had just written a book about the world's best views from toilets and I was feeling nervous. Would I be forever labelled as some kind of a toilet-obsessed freak, mocked, cast out, or, as the Johnny Cash song puts it, *'flushed from the bathroom of your heart'*?

'Bog Standard', 'loodicrous', 'looser', 'panned' by the critics – boy, it was going to be nasty.

But just as I feared the worst, the magic began. A gentleman in Bangalore, India, reads about my search in his morning paper and sends a fantastic photograph of a urinal in the Himalayas; a young British fashion designer promises to 'find a loo with a view if it kills me' on a trip to South America and discovers three; and an architect reads my book and decides to add views to his bathroom designs.

The world was embracing loos with views. It was clear that the journey had only just begun. 'Looser'? I'm proud to be a loo hunter.

Could this be the start of a revolution? Soon, 'toilet pods' will float on the world's most beautiful lakes and rivers; space tourists will sit and marvel at the earth from space; and 3D projectors will be fitted in bathrooms around the world under the tagline 'give your loo a view'. There will be coach tours and loo-hunting holidays, while house prices will rise if the bathroom has a view.

Exciting times lie ahead. However, for the time being, I hope you enjoy this new collection of the world's premier loo views. Thanks so much to everyone who has contacted me at loos@looswithviews.com – this has been an epic communal effort. Together, we have now found loos with views of at least ten UNESCO World Heritage sights, the highest peaks in four out of seven continents, three major sporting arenas, two world-famous communications towers and, perhaps most exciting, a loo with a view of a goat.

A second loos with views book – has the idea 'moved forward' you might ask? Let's just say that this latest collection includes a view from a shower. Enough said, I think.

THE LOOS

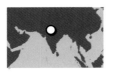

Just outside
Thiksey Buddhist Monastery

Leh, Ladakh, India

View: serene scene, high in the Himalayas while standing

From: Sourav Basu

To: loos@looswithviews.com

Dear Luke,

Congratulations on the successful publication of your new book. The moment I read about it in today's newspaper, I decided to write to you. I will wait for your book to arrive in local book store here in Bangalore, India.

I am sending you a photo taken by me and would be extremely happy if it makes a place in the next edition of your book.

The photo is taken at a peaceful and serene loo located just outside the Thiksey Buddhist Monastery in Leh, Ladakh, India.

Best Regards,

Sourav Basu

NOTES:
Literally the best day of my life.

Beachside Cabana

Mazunte Beach, Mexico

View: Armageddon?

As the Hollywood blockbuster *2012* makes clear, the calendar of the ancient Mayans only runs until the year 2012 when, according to legend, human civilisation will be wiped out.

However, what the film doesn't discuss is that the world will end, or so the story I heard goes anyway, when a giant comet hits earth at the 'Punta Cometa' (Comet Point), Mazunte Beach, Mexico – i.e. here!

What's more, the film neglects to mention that Comet Point (centre frame with tuft sticking up) is visible from this toilet! I'm particularly hurt they left that out. Come 2012 this may well be the best seat in the house – albeit potentially a dangerous one.

NOTES:

By an extraordinary twist of fate Rhiannon May Jones, the loo hunter/holiday maker who unearthed this exciting gem, was travelling with someone whose father collects interesting and historical toilet rolls – the study of which is called cloacopapyrology.

As well as a view of the very spot at which human life on Planet Earth might end, it is also thought possible to see whales and manta rays while seated.

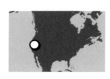

Airship

Floating above California, United States

View: magical – constantly changing before your eyes

Planes, trains, boats, bicycles and airships – toilets on the move are an exciting addition to the 'loos with views' family. They offer a unique, often uplifting, travel experience – and no two visits are ever the same.

I have been told about several, including the Trans Siberian Express; first class on several airlines; the *Waverley* paddle steamer; and a urinal view on the ferry from Portsmouth to the Isle of Wight from which it may be possible to see Osborne House, Queen Victoria's family getaway.

Incredibly, I have also heard tell of ships where the captain's seat doubles as a toilet so that he/she can continue to steer while attending nature's call. I'm not sure that I'd want to eat at that captain's table.

NOTES:

Airship Ventures offer flights to tourists in LA and San Francisco. Potential sightings from their loo include the Hollywood Sign and the Golden Gate Bridge. It may also be possible to see Alcatraz Island in San Francisco Bay – in which case users could look out for the loo in the guard's tower (**A Loo With A View** (**ALWAV**) p22). Now there's an exciting thought.

Of course I haven't found any toilets on bicycles, but I live in hope.

Table Mountain

Upstairs toilet (the one furthest left), Ashanti Lodge, Cape Town, South Africa

View: the mighty Table Mountain

Of all the loos with views in the world, this might well be the most talked about. I have heard of it from at least FOUR separate sources – more than any other loo on the planet.

And it's easy to see why it's so memorable. As well as the magnificent view across the rooftops to Table Mountain, the attention to detail here is staggering:

1. The toilet was moved to allow users to see the view through the window clearly while seated.

2. There's a lovely mosaic on the toilet wall, depicting the mountain and the cable car that takes you to the top.

3. Perhaps most exciting, binoculars are provided (on a chain by the window) to allow users to make the most of this unique opportunity.

NOTES:

Table Mountain is one of the most iconic sights in South Africa. It is charac-
terised by a three-kilometre-long level plateau and offers incredible views,
including Robben Island, where Nelson Mandela was famously imprisoned.

'Pissoir Superstar'

Marisco Tavern, Lundy Island, United Kingdom

View: out to sea, with the mainland in the distance

I didn't dare dream it possible. When I visited the Station Inn, Ribblehead, and marvelled at the sight of trains crossing a magnificent twenty-four-arch viaduct (**ALWAV** p52), I remember thinking that this had to be Britain's finest view from a pub urinal – undisputed.

But now there's a rival to the crown – a new urinal in town.

These two need to get into a ring and sort this thing out. Or perhaps there should be a new TV show to find Britain's best pub urinal and they could go head-to-head for the public vote in the live final? Possible titles: *Pissoir Superstar*, *Stand and Deliver* or *I'm a Urinal, Get in Front of Me*.

NOTES:

This is an open-air, outdoor facility. Users stand before the white wall (pictured in foreground) with a gutter for drainage. Note the water pipe for added proof that this is a urinal.

Owned by The National Trust, Lundy Island lies nineteen kilometres off the coast of north Devon, where the Bristol Channel meets the Atlantic. As well as beautiful loo-views, it offers a variety of activities, including walking and bird-watching.

Cape Cornwall Car Park

Cornwall, United Kingdom

View: man with prominent nose in a bath?

Sadly, this facility has no view from inside (unless you're into soap dispensers). However, with the fantastic Brisons rocks as a backdrop, it arguably boasts the best view while entering/exiting a toilet block in Britain.

The Brisons lie almost two kilometres out to sea. Every year, intrepid swimmers are taken out in fishing boats for the daring 'Brisons Swim' back to shore. It is likely that the rocks were once used as a prison, as the Cornish for prison is brison. Today the rocks are an important breeding ground for sea birds.

The likeness to a man lying in the bath certainly cannot be denied. Many even say that it's *Le Général* himself – the great French leader Charles de Gaulle – on account of the protruding proboscis.

NOTES:

There is also an excellent seasonal snack van in the car park – a 'brew with a view'?

As well as his association with the Brisons, the main airport in Paris is also named after Charles de Gaulle.

Other toilet blocks in car parks with notable views when exiting include the Croagh Patrick car park facility in County Mayo, Ireland (**ALWAV** p10).

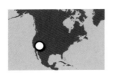

Grand Canyon

Salt Creek Camp, Tonto Trail, Grand Canyon NP, Arizona, United States

View: stunning red rock formations

'Ahhh, Lucas old boy ... just chatting to someone at church – they remember a double-seater with a view across the Grand Canyon ... used it about twenty years ago ... I'll leave it with you ... [My father, December 2008]

Goodness knows I tried. But I've been unable to track down this phenomenal sounding toilet. Dad, I've let you down.

However, I have found one of its neighbours. And, boy, what a toilet it is! Although the view while seated remains a mystery to me, standing users look out across the Grand Canyon National Park to the 'Tower of Set' – the beautiful rock formation on the horizon.

Many of the rocks in this area of the park have Egyptian names. Conspiracy theories abound and some believe there's a more direct link to Ancient Egypt in the canyon with artefacts rumoured to have been discovered within a secret network of caves, which are off-limits to the public.

NOTES:

Some toilets in the park are flown in and out, suspended under helicopters.
Now there's a good idea for a new extreme sport.

Mount Elbrus

The 'Barrels' mountain huts, Caucasus, Russia

View: breathtaking scenery while squatting in the shadow of Elbrus

I searched long and hard to find a loo-view of the scene of a Greek myth. Attempts at Theseus and the Minotaur, The Twelve Labours of Heracles and Icarus and Daedalus sadly proved fruitless. So you can imagine how thrilled I was to learn that Mount Elbrus, the home of no less than TWO loo-views, is a key player in the story of Prometheus. Eureka!

Prometheus is said to have stolen fire from the Gods. As a punishment, Zeus banishes him to Elbrus, where he is chained to a rock and has his liver eaten by an eagle every day – only for it to grow back every night and be eaten again the following day.

At least the view was scenic for poor Prometheus, although can you really appreciate anything when your liver is being repeatedly eaten by an eagle?

NOTES:

Mount Elbrus is the highest mountain in Europe (5,642 metres), although some say that it is in Asia and that the distinction belongs to Mont Blanc (4,810 metres). I don't believe it – mainly because I haven't found any loo-views of Mont Blanc.

Canterbury Cathedral

Ladies Loo, Upstairs in Deeson's British Restaurant,
Canterbury, Kent, United Kingdom

View: the spiritual home of the Church of England and the worldwide
Anglican Communion, as you sit

Following the release of *A Loo with a View*, my friend
Tim Court and I brainstormed ideas for further projects
based around the same theme. They included: a toilet-
based snooker/pool tournament called *A Loo with a
Cue*™; a toilet-based speed-dating business – brand
name *A Loo with a Woo*™; and a detective novel/movie
called *A Loo with a Clue*. There was even *A Loo with
Déjà-vu*, which, in the spirit of Alan Partridge's *A
Partridge Amongst the Pigeons* idea, was 'just a title'.

Sadly, none of our ideas seems to have materialised.
That is, until now. Ladies and gentlemen, I am proud to
present *A Loo with a Pew* (toilets with views of churches).

NOTES:

Fear not. Despite frosted glass on the lower window, the cathedral is visible through
the upper while seated – and also looks heavenly when flood-lit at night.

Canterbury Cathedral dates from AD 597, when St Augustine, sent by the Pope as
a missionary, established his seat (a.k.a. cathedra) in Canterbury. The cathedral is
symbolic of the tension between religion and state – in 1170, Archbishop Thomas
Beckett was famously murdered inside by four knights of King Henry II.

BT Tower

Heights Bar, St Georges Hotel, Langham Place, London

View: one of two major communications towers now known to be visible from urinals

As I dried my hands and walked towards the elevator, to descend from the Jin Mao Building back to the streets of Shanghai, I wondered with sadness whether this might just be the last time I ever saw a major communications tower from a urinal (**ALWAV** p62).

Imagine my delight, then, when news reached me that right in the heart of London – under my very nose – sat a urinal with a view of the iconic BT Tower. The dream lives on.

BT was also excited to hear of the find: 'This really is tremendous news,' said a spokesman.

NOTES:

The BT Tower has been part of the London skyline since the 1960s and was officially opened to the public in May 1966 by Tony Benn, MP and Sir Billy Butlin, whose leisure company (Butlins) operated a revolving restaurant at the top.

Also visible from the loo (in the distance with a 90-degree neck twist) is St Paul's Cathedral, as you look out across Soho and Bloomsbury towards the river (more content for *A Loo with a Pew* – damn, it's going to be good).

As well as the view, this loo also boasts a working shoe-polishing machine.

Refuge de Lagazuoi

Dolomites Mountains, Italy

View: through the window from the peak of Mount Lagazuoi
(with radiator for added comfort)

Of all the various genres of 'loo-view', my favourite is 'historical'. We spend an awful lot of our lives locked in bathrooms and, once in a while, it's refreshing to walk into a toilet and be transported back into history.

And here, located at a splendid mountain inn high in the Dolomites, is a classic example. As you sit gazing out of the window, it's incredible to think that beneath you, within the bowels of the mountain, are tunnels (now an open-air museum) dating back to the First World War.

They were dug by the Austro-Hungarian and Italian armies, as they waged a ferocious war in the Dolomites. Both armies set up bases inside the mountain, attempting to destroy the other with dynamite.

NOTES:

I have taken the liberty of 'tagging' the photo, to show just how impressive the location of this loo is.

Other loos associated with wartime tunnels include one at Dover Castle in the UK (**ALWAV** p26). Both sets of tunnels are open to the public. Lagazuoi can be reached on foot or by cable car/chair lift.

loo

Just Below the Peak of Mount Rysy

Mountain Chalet Toilet, High Tatra Mountains, Slovakia

View: multi-faceted – spectacular while queuing, out through a
heart-shaped hole and the loo is a view in itself

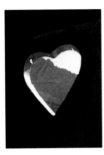

It wouldn't be an exaggeration to describe this toilet as a
cocoon of joy. Perched high in the High Tatra Mountains,
here is a loo that is high on life. If it ordered an alcoholic
drink, it'd be a 'Grin and Tonic'!!!!! Raucous!!!!!

Painted decorations include: a smiling sun, a cute
bird, a handsome snail, floating balloons and a cheeky
toadstool with its tongue sticking out.

And if that wasn't enough, the inside is also decorated
and features a heart-shaped hole – no doubt for
ventilation, as well as a reminder for us all to view the
world with joy and love in our hearts.

NOTES:

The popular Rysy Mountain sits on the border between Poland and Slovakia and is
Poland's highest peak.

There used to be a border crossing on the summit. However, this was shut down in
2007, when a border cooperation scheme was adopted between the two countries.

Baños Fantásticos

Ladies Loo, Café Mirador, Sucre, Bolivia

View: through slats in door or with door open, the historic World Heritage City of Sucre

GABZ AND MEL VOL 1 – Gabz finds her first loo-view

'I was getting pretty sick of looking for toilets,' revealed Gabz's travelling companion Mel.

'She was completely obsessed and I was actually thinking of ditching her. Then, one day, we're sitting at a café in the hills above Sucre, Bolivia. No surprise, Gabz announces that she's "just popping to the toilets" – she'd been twice already that morning, I knew what was going on. Suddenly: "*Loo with a view! Loo with a view! Loo with a view!*" The screams went on for ages, echoing out over the city.'

Mel didn't question Gabz again after that. What a moment – and what a loo.

NOTES:

Named after the independence leader Antonio José de Sucre, Sucre is often regarded as the birthplace and epicentre of the nineteenth-century independence movement in the Spanish colonies.

Gabz (a.k.a. Gabrielle Carter) is a young British fashion designer who heard about my search from a friend at a line-dancing event. She and Mel spent four months travelling in South America in 2009.

A Loo Set Free

View: captured from the urinal, the Matterhorn as seen through broken frosted glass

For anyone trying to find loos with great views, the sight of frosted glass is a constant thorn in the dream, leading to countless 'what ifs' and 'if onlys'.

And so I was heartened to see this astonishing photograph. A loo finds its view – a loo is set free – and with it, gone is the heartache of countless frost-induced disappointments.

But is there something bigger going on here? Could this have been a calculated act? Is there a global movement of undercover activists out there, dedicated to the eradication of frosted glass in public toilets?

It might sound ridiculous, but I've done some investigating and can reveal that the domain name 'frost-sucks.org' is unavailable. The plot thickens?

NOTES:

No it doesn't. I totally made that up.

The author does not encourage vandalism of any kind.

'Cock-a-Doodle-Loo'

Cock View Manor, Pristor, Somerset, United Kingdom*

View: enormous gold plated church cockerel

Massive news from Cock View Manor! If preliminary plans are approved, this loo will soon be turned 180 degrees to face a new floor-to-ceiling window made entirely of one-way glass. What's more, the uplifting sound of male voice choirs will be piped into the bathroom on a continuous loop. What a truly exciting experience it will be, like being serenaded from heaven.

But for the time being, it still remains a pretty good loo-view. It doesn't get much better than seeing Europe's largest church cockerel (as claimed by local residents) from a toilet. Measuring in at 1.8m by 1.5m, the whopping bird has sat proud on top of the village church for around 200 years. It must have seen a thing or two in its time.

NOTES:

Seeing the cockerel while using the loo currently requires users (male) to stand to the right, with knees bent and neck strained in order to line up with the only available gap in the tree. It certainly isn't easy, but you do get to see the (reputed) largest church cockerel in Europe from a toilet.

*Address changed to protect identity of owners

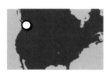

Loos 7 & 11

Mount Baker, Washington, United States

View: either a sensational view from the mountain or your climbing buddy's back

In 1792, a British ship commanded by explorer George Vancouver was mapping the Pacific Northwest Coast of America. As the ship sat anchored in Dungeness Bay, 3rd Lieutenant Joseph Baker spotted a rather impressive mountain. Mount Baker was born.

By an extraordinary twist of fate, the gentleman who captured this fantastic image on Mount Baker recalls seeing the 'twinkling lights of the city of Vancouver' (named after Baker's commander, of course) from a toilet on the mountain.

Sensational historical toileting!

NOTES:

The numbers on the loos reveal that Mount Baker is home to at least eleven toilets – no doubt all with views. To use them all in one day would be challenging on so many levels.

Mount Baker had been known to the indigenous population for centuries. The Spanish also 'discovered' it in 1790.

The position of the seat hinges proves that the toilets face the same way. Assuming both are occupied simultaneously, I'm undecided which I'd be more comfortable using!

Melbourne Cricket Ground

35th Floor, Sofitel, Melbourne, Australia

View: the famous MCG (easily seen from sinks – neck twist required from urinals)

Mentioned in guide books and famous throughout Melbourne, this loo has become a tourist stop in its own right. But a visit is also a great way to see the city – visible from it is the State Parliament, the Treasury and, perhaps most exciting, the Melbourne Cricket Ground, also the symbolic home of Australian Rules football.

Funnily enough, I was informed by a fan of the Aussie Rules team the 'London Swans' (she was also a member of the sister netball team, the 'Swanettes') that the Ladies has a similarly impressive view from the cubicle nearest the window. She suspected that I was using the loo-book story as an elaborate ruse and that I was actually a spy from local rivals the 'West London Wildcats'. Cover maintained...

NOTES:

Other major grounds known to be visible from toilets are:

1. Lords Cricket Ground (**ALWAV** p32)

2. PCN Park, home of the Pittsburgh Pirates (overleaf)

I have also heard of a loo *inside* the MCG with a view of the pitch, but sadly this remains unconfirmed, for now.

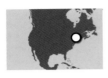

Room 1023
Renaissance Hotel, Pittsburgh, Pennsylvania,
United States

View: a dream come true – live Major League Baseball, while seated

Following the release of the 1994 hit movie *Four Weddings and a Funeral*, demand for the 'Elizabeth I Four Poster Suite' at The Crown in Amersham – the location of Hugh Grant and Andie McDowell's first love scene – is said to have sky-rocketed.

The same is bound to happen here. From now on, 1023 is sure to be the hottest room in town.

And what a view it is – across the Allegheny River into the home of the Pittsburgh Pirates. It's even possible to see the home plate and all four bases – making the view particularly special on game days.

Also visible is the Roberto Clemente Bridge, named after the former Pirates' right fielder, who was tragically killed in a plane crash on New Year's Eve, 1972, trying to deliver aid to Nicaragua following an earthquake.

NOTES:

It is only natural to compare this loo to the toilet with a view of the MCG (see previous entry). Unlike Melbourne, it offers a view inside of the stadium (1–0). However, it requires users to rent a room (1–1). It is swings and roundabouts in the loo-view game.

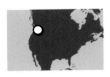

Bucket Race

Conconully Outhouse Races, Washington, United States

View: inside of bucket

With hearts pumping they run – pushing a purpose-built, three-sided wooden outhouse on skis through the snow with buckets on their heads. A third team member bravely sits inside, shouting directions over the deafening noise of the crowd. This is the Conconully Bucket Race. This is the greatest race on earth.

There has been outhouse racing at Conconully for at least a quarter of a century. Outhouses are raced head-to-head down the main street in a number of divisions (not all races involve buckets). According to the rules of competition, all outhouses must be equipped with a toilet seat and toilet roll on a hanger and all riders must wear helmets.

NOTES:

Outhouse racing is alive and well in the United States. There are a number of different races in a number of different states – some on skis, some on wheels.

Although not technically 'real' toilets, they offer a unique adrenalin-filled loo-view experience for the rider and so are worthy of inclusion.

Outhouse racing is yet to catch on in Britain – although I have been lucky enough to witness a number of 'duck races' down village streams, using plastic ducks.

INTERM

ISSION

a.k.a. toilet break

*Exciting sneak preview of nominees
for the forthcoming (fictional)*

LooView Awards

(LAVs)

Best view
while standing

W.C

Desert WC, Close to the Ksar Ghilane Oasis,
Sahara Desert, Tunisia

*Best view
while seated*
in an outdoor setting

'The Chateau', Wolwedans Lodge, NamibRand Nature
Reserve, Namibia.

Best view
while entering,
exiting or queuing

Santa Cruz Trek, Bolivia

Best view
of a loo

Croagh Patrick, County Mayo, Ireland

Baños Públicos in Los Flamencos
Laguna Miñique, Los Flamencos National Reserve,
Atacama Desert, Chile

View: the stunning Miñique Lagoon and Miñique Volcano

In 2009, a couple from London embarked on an epic journey together, vowing before they left to find a loo with a view.

Their first challenge was to cycle across America – an epic 6,700-kilometre road trip. They 'thought of me' in every toilet they entered. But nothing.

Next stop was South America, where they were on the verge of tracking down a loo with a view in Los Glaciares National Park, Argentina, before being thwarted at the last minute by a landslide.

Just days before they were due to return home, 'empty-handed', it happened. Some things are just meant to be.

NOTES:

This loo symbolises the spirit of adventure and dedication to the cause that has made this book possible.

The loo offers magical views while exiting. It may also offer a view through the door while seated (as pictured). However, this requires the door to be left open (risky if there's a queue) and for users to lean forward with a twist neck – not the most dignified manoeuvre, but technically possible.

How cute is the ventilation chimney?!

Scilly Isles

Dolphin House, Tresco, Isles of Scilly, United Kingdom

View: across to Old Grimsby Quay and Islands beyond

The scene of a blissful family holiday, I had long dreamed of seeing a 'loo with a view' on the Isles of Scilly. There were exciting rumours of three-sided huts looking out to sea, but the island's loo-views remained tantalisingly out of reach.

Finally, it happened – and the wait was certainly worth it.

The 'Scillies' sit in the Atlantic Ocean, some 45 kilometres off Lands End – the most westerly point in Britain. Tresco is one of five inhabited islands in the archipelago. Thanks to a sub-tropical climate, the famous Abbey Gardens are able to thrive on the island, filled with exotic plants from around the world.

The Scillies are known to have the smallest football league in the world – one pitch and two clubs, who are said to play each other seventeen times every season, competing for two cups as well as the league title.

NOTES:

You will be pleased to know that this view is also visible from the bath.
On a clear day the Scillies are visible from Cape Cornwall (**Good Loo Hunting (GLH)** p20). Thanks to the Tresco Estate, who own and rent Dolphin House as a holiday cottage.

Nomadic Loo Tent

Annapurna Foothills, Himalayas, Nepal

View: great start to the day – captured just after dawn, the Annapurna range including sacred Machapuchare

Nomadic in nature, loo tents offer a constantly changing view. Like the 'Littlest Hobo', of TV dog fame, they 'keep on moving on', don't like to be tied down (metaphorically at least) and bring relief to those they meet.

Although it has no view from inside, this tent must have been pitched in some pretty exciting places in its time. And none more so than here – pegged down at 1,600 metres above sea level in the foothills of the Annapurna Range in the Himalayas.

Machapuchare is pictured directly above the tent. Also known as Fish-tail Mountain on account of its double summit (which looks a bit like a fish-tail) the mountain is now closed to climbers, as it's regarded as sacred to the Hindu god Shiva. A British expedition got close to the top in 1957. However, they stopped just shy because they had promised not to set foot on the summit.

NOTES:

You could produce a whole book, or even feature-length documentary, about the life and times of a loo tent – possible title: *In Search of the Perfect Pitch*. Surely a winner?

MAX

View: a train that looks like an animal?

Tokyo is a veritable hotbed for urinal views. A city of limited space, where things are built upwards, it offers ideal conditions for spectacular toileting.

But of all the urinals in all of Tokyo, this has the potential to deliver something truly extraordinary. With a clear view of the railway line near Tokyo Station, it might just be possible to stand before it and see my favourite bullet train – the E4 Series 'MAX' (Multi Amenity express).

It's a double-decker and, of course, travels at lightning speed (max 240km/h). But, best of all, it looks a bit like an animal. I think a rampaging bison (others say carp fish). I have heard stories of tourists arriving in Tokyo and heading straight to the station, just to see it. This is the way trains ought to be – as exciting as it must have felt when the first steam locomotives were built in the nineteenth century.

NOTES:

I have deliberately not researched whether the 'MAX' travels on this particular line. I am not sure I could handle it if not.

Hiroshima Peace Memorial Park

Hiroshima, Honshu, Japan

View: the world famous Hiroshima Peace Memorial, or 'A-Dome'

It was once the Hiroshima Industrial Promotions Hall. Today it's a World Heritage site and one of the world's most iconic structures. The A-Dome stands as a memorial to those killed by the atomic bomb of 6 August 1945. Now it promotes peace.

The bomb detonated 580 metres above ground and just 150 metres away from the Dome – causing instant and unparalleled death and destruction to the city. An estimated 140,000 were killed, many after the initial explosion as a result of radiation poisoning, and some 70 per cent of Hiroshima's buildings were destroyed.

Somehow the Dome stayed standing. Hiroshima was rebuilt around it and today the Dome is a constant reminder of the devastating cost of nuclear war.

NOTES:

Hiroshima became a 'peace memorial city' and, as such, every time a country authorises the detonation of a nuclear device, the Mayor of Hiroshima writes to its leader in protest.

Japan surrendered shortly after the bombings of Hiroshima and of Nagasaki, three days later. Some argue that the bombs were justified as they brought the war to a speedy end, ultimately resulting in fewer deaths than if Japan had continued to fight on.

Kilimanjaro

Karanga Valley, Mount Kilimanjaro, Tanzania

View: amazing – it's the highest point in Africa

Progress in the 'Seven Summits' loo-view challenge (the seven summits are the highest peaks in each of the seven continents):

- Africa, Kilimanjaro ✓
- Antarctica, Vinson Massif
  Rumours of an ice toilet, accessible by plane, at base camp with view of the peak
  (unconfirmed)
- Australasia, Kosciuszko
  Have read that a toilet has been built on the peak
  (unconfirmed)
- Asia, Everest ✓
  At the Tengboche Monastery, Nepal (ALWAV p14)

- Europe, Elbrus ✓ ✓
  Double tick!
  (ALWAV p40 and GLH p24)
- North America, McKinley ✓
  Tentative tick. Loo at 4,328 metres. View while sitting is of Mount Foraker. However, view while standing is unknown and may include the peak
  (ALWAV p50)
- South America, Aconcagua
  Sadly no tick.

NOTES:

4/7 (albeit with one tentative tick).

Oh geez – I think I might know too much about toilets.

To reach all seven summits is a major achievement in mountaineering. Likewise, visiting a loo with a view of each peak would be considered a major achievement in toilet hunting.

In 2009, a group of celebrities climbed Kilimanjaro for the BBC Comic Relief appeal. It's very possible that Take That singer Gary Barlow has at least seen these toilets.

Shower
Backpacker Hostel, Cusco, Peru

View: the historic capital of the Incan Empire as you exfoliate

GABZ AND MEL VOL 2

From: Gabrielle Carter

To: <u>Luke Barclay</u>

Cc: Mel

Subject: Ducha with a Viewsha?

Dear Luke,

Don't suppose you're at all interested in views from showers are you? My fiancé once peed in one, if that helps?

Hope to hear from you soon.

Best wishes,

Gabz

NOTES:

A view from a shower!? Talk about pushing the boundaries. What's next? Bidets?

I have also heard tell of a shower in Uganda with a view of the source of the Nile – the greatest hair wash on Earth?

Cusco is a World Heritage City and the historical capital of Peru. It was once the centre of the Inca Empire, which spanned much of western South America in the fifteenth and sixteenth centuries, before the arrival of the Spanish conquistadors.

Halfway Guesthouse

Tiger Leaping Gorge, Yunnan Province, China

View: gaze across the gorge while squatting with the Yangtze River rushing below

While it remains possible that Gary Barlow has seen the loos featured on Kilimanjaro, we know for SURE that a television legend has visited these. Broadcast in 2004, Michael Palin travelled through Tiger Leaping Gorge for his BBC *Himalayas* series – stopping at the Halfway Guesthouse and passing comment on the phenomenal loo-view.

And what a view it is. To enjoy it for a prolonged period certainly requires strong legs. But I think it's worth training for in advance. This is an extraordinary canyon – 15km long with sheer 2,000m cliffs. Legend has it that a tiger once leapt across the river to evade a hunter, which is how the gorge gets its name.

NOTES:

The loo is advertised on rocks on the trail: '24 hour hot shower, delicious pancake, homemade apple pie and scenic toilet view'. What a combination.

Measuring in at just shy of 6,500 kilometres, the Yangtze River is the third longest in the world, behind the Nile and the Amazon.

Banks of the Zambezi
Old Mondoro Bush Camp,
Lower Zambezi National Park, Zambia
View: 'trunk-tastic'! Best see at 'tusk'?

With a clear sight of the Zambezi while seated or from the sinks, today this loo is a great place for toilet-based game spotting – elephant, hippo and croc are all said to have been seen from it.

However, had the loo existed in the nineteenth century, users might also have seen Dr Livingstone as he travelled down the river on his way to discovering Victoria Falls.

In fact, given that there's also a loo on Livingstone Island with a view of the falls (**ALWAV** p24), one could technically now journey in the great man's footsteps, stopping at loos along the way.

Mountain Hut

High above Mayrhofen, Tirol, Austria

View: voyeuristic goat

Updated list of reported animal sightings from loos:

1. African elephants, crossing river, Zambia (**GLH** p70)

2. Hippopotami, wallowing in river, Zambia (**ALWAV** p74)

3. Crocodile, lurking in river, Zambia (anecdotal, 2 sources)

4. Urban fox cubs, frolicking on garden lawn, London (anecdotal)

5. Green Indian ring-necked parakeets, perching, India (**ALWAV** p56)

6. Southern right whales, mating, South Africa (anecdotal)

7. Marmots, looking cute, United States (anecdotal, 2 sources)

8. Black Noddy terns, mating and rearing young in nests, Great Barrier Reef (**ALWAV** p30)

9. Goat, staring, Austria (this page)

NOTES:

This might be the closest we have come to finding a loo-view of the scene of a famous masterpiece, with Marc Chagall often including goats in his paintings. For example, the 'violin-playing goat' discussed in the movie *Notting Hill*.

Theories abound as to the significance of goats for Chagall. One is that he was referring to the Jewish Day of Atonement, when a goat was sent out into the wilderness to atone for man's sins.

Or maybe he just liked goats?

Windmill Village

Zaanse Schans, Zaandam, Netherlands

View: windmills

The banks of the River Zaan were once teeming with activity. This was the heartland of early-industrial Holland – many hundreds of mills, harnessing the natural power of the wind to produce everything from corn to cloth to cocoa.

Today, Zaanse Schans – an open-air museum and conservation area – is one of Holland's top tourist destinations. As well as windmills, historic shipyards and clog-making demos, sights include this traditional toilet, which overhangs the river – taking you back to life before the flush.

NOTES:

Sanitation has moved on in modern-day Holland. But today, in many parts of the world, communities don't have access to even this basic kind of toilet facility. Some 2.5 billion people are said to live without access to adequate sanitation, leading to unnecessary disease and death.

Charities such as the UK-based Pump Aid are working towards breaking the toilet taboo and improving this dire situation. See www.pumpaid.org for more information about their work.

This view rivals 'goat from urinal' for the loo-view which most resembles a famous work of art. It's reminiscent of a number of paintings by French artist Claude Monet, including his *Windmills near Zaandam*.

Monks En Masse

Buddhist Monastery, Tibet

View: a rare find – many monks can utilise simultaneously

At least ten outdoor toilets, lined up in a row at a monastery in Tibet.

One word ...

AWESOME.

NOTES:

Other notable examples of 'communal toileting' include:

1. The loos of the Roman legionaries: ruins can be seen at Ephesus in Turkey, Sabratha and Leptis Magna in Libya, and Hadrian's Wall (particularly at Housesteads Fort) in Northumbria, UK.

2. A 'three-holer' at Kelmscott Manor, Gloucestershire, UK, the country home of the nineteenth-century artist, poet and socialist William Morris. The house is open to the public, but sadly you're not allowed to use the loo.

3. Incredibly, King Louis XIV of France is said to have announced his betrothal from his commode – every girl's dream? Both he and Louis XIII gave audience while 'seated', with Louis XIII said to have had a commode built into his throne.

It's not surprising that a number of the communal toilets found in this search have been located at Buddhist monasteries or temples, as Buddhism is a religion that encourages us to live without ego.

Antarctica

Portable Latrine, Hovgaard Island

View: in 24-hour daylight, the silent magnificent beauty of the Antarctic

OCCUPIED

It feels inappropriate to interrupt the unique and personal experience of sitting alone, looking out at the edge of Earth's last untouched wilderness.

But I will anyway.

This toilet has been described as 'the eighth wonder of the world'. However, of the original seven wonders of the ancient world it may be possible to see the only surviving member, the Great Pyramid at Giza, from a toilet. I received news from an air-hostess that first-class passengers (who often have windows in their toilets) can potentially enjoy a loo-view of the pyramids shortly before landing at Cairo. My loo spies are everywhere!

NOTES:

However, she did point out that the 'fasten seat belt' sign might well be on by this stage, making such an endeavour dangerous and probably illegal.

Valle Gran Rey (STATUS 'PROBABLE')

Mirador César Manrique, La Gomera, Canary Islands

View: 'look-out' over the Valle Gran Rey

Despite the absence of a 'loo' picture to prove that this is a bona fide loo-view, I have it on good authority that both the Ladies and Gents offer the same spectacular view across the Valle Gran Rey on the island of La Gomera.

However, I am aware that my reputation as a finder of loo-views is on the line here, so I can confirm that I have discovered a second source. The *Guardian* newspaper, no less: 'This place would win "the world's best view from a lavatory award" hands down,' wrote Jonathan Lee in 2005.

That's good enough for me, although I hope to have demonstrated that there's some pretty stiff competition out there for such an award.

NOTES:

I am aware that Jonathan Lee is male, so this doesn't necessarily confirm the view from the Ladies, but as Austin Powers once said: 'throw me a frickin' bone here'.

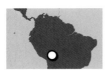

Isla del Sol

Lake Titicaca, Copacabana, Peru

View: through holes in door, or with door open, gaze in awe across Lake Titicaca to Bolivia

GABZ AND MEL VOL 3

From: Luke Barclay

To: <u>Gabrielle Carter</u>

Cc: Mel

Subject: Loo Mission

Don't suppose you guys are going anywhere near Copacabana are you? There have been sightings...

Details to follow, should you choose to accept this daring mission...

Kind regards,

Luke

NOTES:

And so it was that with no money to stay on the island and their ride back to the mainland departing in minutes, Gabz and Mel continued their desperate search of the Isla del Sol. 'Look – Inca ruins!' said Mel, as they ran. 'Are they a toilet Mel!? NOT interested ...' replied Gabz. They were about to throw in the towel when they saw it. But elation turned to despair – the door was padlocked! A group of travellers practising 'laughter yoga' (or maybe they were laughing at Gabz and Mel) offered to go and get the keys. But there was no time. This was snatch and grab – loo hunting on the edge.

The beautiful Isla del Sol is accessible from Copacabana and is famous for Inca ruins.

Inca Trail

Andes, Peru

View: not Machu Picchu

~~~~~~

When I set out on my quest to find the world's best loos with views, I penned a list of views that I wanted to find. It included 'Mount Everest, preferably peak', 'large game e.g. elephant', 'the northern lights', 'the earth from space' and 'the scene of a Constable painting'. Happily, many have now been found, photographed and crossed off. Some, however, remain elusive.

And none more so than 'a loo with a view' of the 'lost city' of Machu Picchu. But at least we're getting closer and are on the Inca Trail – the ancient path to Machu Picchu, which winds its way to the city via mountain passes, cloud forests and Inca ruins.

Although we are yet to find the 'golden toilet', a friend of mine claims to have seen Machu Picchu while squatting in the grass next to the trail and says that the ancient city was framed by a rainbow! A once-in-a-lifetime experience...

NOTES:

Of all the characters in *Star Wars*, I think this loo looks most like an Ewok, or R2D2.

A Loo With a Cockatoo

Upstairs Bathroom, Budgie Cottage, Budgie

View: unknown

In 2008, I was privileged to see a pair of green Indian ring-necked parakeets from the toilet window of a former Indian palace (**ALWAV** p56). But not in my wildest dreams did I imagine that just a few months later I would be feasting my eyes on this astonishing scene.

Thanks to Australian-based animal trainer Trieste Visier for sending in this extraordinary image. I acknowledge that it's not technically a 'loo with a view'. But it is a loo with a budgie perched on top and that's good enough for me.

NOTES:

Trieste photographs budgerigars getting up to everyday antics, e.g. skateboarding, playing tennis and playing the guitar.

The budgie is clearly well trained and is doing a tremendous job of appearing constipated – an affliction said to be shared by Martin Luther, the father of the sixteenth-century Protestant Reformation. In 2004, archaeologists in Germany discovered his loo, where he reputedly spent many hours in quiet contemplation.

It was a toilet that helped change the world. Somehow, I think this one might change the world too.

Trieste's budgies can be seen at **www.skateboardingbudgies.blogspot.com**.

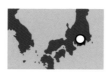

A View That Needs a Loo

Summit of Mount Fuji, Honshū, Japan

View: NOT from a toilet – 'Fuji-San' casts its imperious shadow out west over Japan

Having climbed through the night to make it in time for sunrise, the summit of Mount Fuji was filled with glorious surprises – vending machines selling hot and cold drinks, a noodle restaurant, even a post office.

After enjoying a hot coffee from a can, purchased from a machine at nearly 4,000 metres, and visiting the loo which I had travelled thousands of kilometres to see, I decided to walk round the crater rim before starting my descent. It takes about an hour and is a moment of calm in an otherwise gruelling, albeit extraordinary, experience.

About halfway round, on the west side, the most excited man I have ever seen called me over and beckoned me up a ladder to a small viewing platform. PHEN-OM-EN-AL!

NOTES:

An awe-inspiring view, but where's the toilet to see it from?!
Can't believe that was the first thing that crossed my mind.

It's included to illustrate the highs and lows of hunting for loo-views.

(See **ALWAV** p4 for more on the summit toilet.)

Chrysler Building (STATUS 'MYTHICAL')
Manhattan Island, New York City, New York,
United States

View: 360-degree panoramas from golden toilet?

On a trip to New York City, I happened upon an urban legend. At the very top of the Chrysler Building and accessible only by a series of ladders (some even say it's inside the spire), supposedly sits a toilet! The story goes that the famous industrialist Walter P. Chrysler wanted the highest room in his building – once the tallest in the world – to be a toilet. Perhaps so he could sit and look out at the world he had conquered.

Following a chance meeting at a wedding, the plot thickened. Although most of the Chrysler Building is closed to the public, incredibly, someone knew someone who had seen this mythical latrine. They report that not only does it exist, but it also has 360-degree views of New York and is made of solid gold!

NOTES:

Part of me doesn't even want to know. What if it isn't true? However, if these incredible reports are confirmed, this would surely be the ultimate loo with a view. My search would be over and I could rest easy.

What a place it would be to end a journey.

Acknowledgements

Thanks so much to everyone who has contacted me with loo leads and photos, and to everyone who has allowed me to include their photographs in this collection – please see photo credits for individual names.

In no particular order, special thanks to: Anna, Matt and Ollie Cardy; Gabrielle Carter; Melanie Erlam; Jon Hawkins; Samuel Kashima; Mum and Dad, Sarah and Paul Barclay (Dad, you've been incredible, thanks from 'Lucas Old Boy'); Sourav Basu; Tom Henson; the owners of Cock View Manor; David Briese; Rhiannon May Jones; anyone involved in Outhouse Racing and whoever thought it up; Virgin Books, especially Ed Faulkner, Davina Russell, Sophia Brown and Toby Clarke; The Tresco Estate; Alice Barclay; Ashanti Lodge Cape Town; budgies in general; The Landmark Trust; Grace Bastidas; Jacob Jones; Sarah and Matt Law; Lindsey Kucharski; the team at frost-sucks.org; Old Mondoro Bush Camp; Max, George and Bella; Tim Court; Wolwedans Lodge, Namibia; Airship Ventures; James Spackman; Lizzi Carter; The Renaissance Hotel, Pittsburgh; and many more…

Good loo hunting to one and all. I'd love to hear about any finds:
loos@looswithviews.com

Photo Credits

4–5	© Valerie McDougall
6–7	© Valerie McDougall
8–9	© Luke Barclay
10–11	© Sourav Basu
12–13	© Rhiannon May Jones*
14–15	© Airship Ventures, Inc.
16–17	© Samantha Cope
18	© Anna Cardy
19	© Robin Oakley
20–21	© Luke Barclay
22–23	© Jindrich Capek
24–25	© Chris R. Stokes
26–27	© Luke Barclay
28–29	© Luke Barclay
30–31	© Peter Brookes
32–33	© Carol Hill
34–35	© Gabrielle Carter
36–37	© David Hanmer
38–39	© Anna Cardy
40–41	© Burt Rosen
42–43	© Andy Cunningham
44–45	© Grace Bastidas
47	© Jennifer Swayne
50	© Maurizio Pichierri
51	© Tracey Garrett
52	© David Briese
53	© Luke Barclay
54–55	© Sarah Law
56–57	© Jane Thatcher
58–59	© Richard Bottle
60	© Luke Barclay
61	© Henry Readhead
63	© Sam Barclay

65	© Jacob Jones
66–67	© Gabrielle Carter
68–69	© David McLerran
70–71	© Lana De Villiers
73	© David Hanmer
74–75	© Terry Langhorn
76–77	© Diana van der Bij & Bart-Willem van Leeuwen
78–79	© David Briese
81	© Roger and Rosemary Tranter
82–83	© Gabrielle Carter
84–85	© Rhiannon May Jones*
86	© Luke Barclay
87	© Trieste Visier
88–89	© Luke Barclay
91	© Luke Barclay

* rhiannonmayphotography.co.uk

The Loo List

The Loo List [cont.]